Take The Lead

Take The Lead

How Top Leaders Are Tapping Into Power
By Overcoming Frustrations

TRACEY JONES

ISBN: 978-1-7377517-0-0

Front Cover design/artist/Image: Sophisticated Press LLC
Printed in the United States of America

Published By Tracey Jones
Publishing Consultant

SP

SOPHISTICATED
PRESS

ACKNOWLEDGMENTS

This book is dedicated to you. I hope that you find joy and inspiration in overcoming your frustration. The most significant investment made is in you.

Table of Contents

Introduction

Today you get a chance to receive this reading because of gratefulness. Long before I had what I wanted, I acted as if I had everything I needed. I became more grateful for what I was already accountable for; as a black male growing up on the south side of Monroe, Louisiana. Early in life my step father taught me about the LICS system. Locate the problem, isolate and separate the problem, confirm that you have identified the problem, then solve the problem using logic. He noted the law has no sympathy for your ignorance of it.

I have two strikes against me. First strike, I'm a man. Second strike, I'm a black man. He noted that I would have to work three times as hard as the next man to succeed. I learned at an early age; your circle of friends would determine your future therefore, I never hung with crowds just to say I have friends.

To this day, I have the same circle of friends. We all met playing junior high school football. As adults we have all gone our separate ways; however, we remain close. Anytime we come together it's like the day we first met. These are the same guys that call my mom their mom, and I call their mom, my mom.

I experienced a great share of pain, trauma, and heartache at an early age. My mom disciplined me at age nine or ten for acting out at a family members house. Afterwards I told my mother I wanted to stay with my dad. My mother dropped me off to my dad, she thought he would keep me a couple days and bring me back home. To my surprise, dad called the police on my mother for child abuse. As soon as mom and I met him at his mother's house. I got what I wanted, I got a chance to stay with my dad.

Things didn't go as expected. My mom lost custody of my brother and I after spending thousands of dollars on multiple lawyers. After spending time talking with my aunt, mom soon gave up. She put her trust in God that we would be okay. After staying with dad for about 2 years, one Saturday morning he told us to pack our clothes and everything we had. I asked him, "Where are we going?" We ended up at my grandmother on my mom's side's house. Dad's words to her were, "Tell your daughter she can have her kids. They messed my marriage up, I no longer want them." There I was standing next to my black Next bike with my name in gold lettering, my brother's silver bike with his name in blue lettering and two trash bags of clothes. "I no longer want them". That constantly plays over and over in my head. That was my first heartbreak from my dad, the man I saw as my hero. My world shattered. My mom and my step father took us back in. They never brought up what we've been through, they immediately took over, making sure we were off to a happy start. Shortly after being back home with my mom, I experienced my first murder. I was 12 years old, in junior high school getting dressed. I heard loud noises coming from outside, so my brother and I started to look out the window of my grandmother's bedroom.

I witnessed a white car reversing out of the driveway, a male was standing next to the white car as it drove backward. As the female puts the car into drive, four shots ring out— boom,boom,boom,boom. The white vehicle rolled forward as it crashed into the front of the neighbor's porch. Minutes later we went outside as we started to see other neighbors out. The body slumped over on the steering wheel while brains were lying on the seat. That day was frightening to me, it was scary. After experiencing that situation along with everything prior, I began to act out for love and attention, I never took anything serious. My mom considered me a loose cannon while growing up because I didn't understand my worth and my value.

This affected many relationships I had with women, friends, and family. I would easily give my love and trust, then I would find a way to sabotage the relationship to keep from being hurt. When things are going great in my life, I would do something to hurt the people I'm experiencing the happiness with, which would result in me hurting myself overall. I always ended up with leadership positions, whether that was at home, sports, or work. I knew at an early age I had a gift of leadership. I knew at some point in life I would have to live out my calling. I stopped making excuses for my actions. I took accountability for my life. I became the leader of my life. Life is a journey of self-discovery. There is a purpose and a plan for every soul. Through my journey of self-discovery, I realized success wasn't a secret. They're proven steps, strategies, and techniques that lead to success. The human mind is powerful. We attract what we are. I challenged myself daily to study something and someone. I realized as I grew, others around me grew, seeing growth in others forced me to continue to grow.

I realized people pay more attention to your actions and deeds than what you say. I started at sonic drive-in when I was 16 years old as a cook, at $5.15 minimum wage. With year's of learning and cultivating the system I was promoted to an assistant manager with continued years of hard work lead to me becoming a co manager. By the age of 23 years old, I managed to grind my way to an operating partner. I took it upon myself to learn from every manager I worked with. I studied concepts, methods and techniques. Once I learned about the results expected, I became focused on executing and achieving those results. I realized my drive and dedication put me in a position to take the lead in my life. It was no longer about how great I am at my job, it became about how well I can achieve and excel.

Everyone wants to feel loved, accepted, and appreciated. I created positive environments that allows positive energy to flow in the atmosphere . It wasn't about me, It was about my guests. My team is a reflection of me. Profit is a reflection of your productivity. Missing profit and results can be frustrating; however, I began to realize that I'm in control of my employee's actions. I'm not able to control their actions directly, so I am faced with certain decisions. What could I do differently if I can't be the only one to provide excellent service all day? My mind instantly reverted to sports. If the team is getting beat by three touchdowns, do you see the coach come in and make a play? If Shaquille O'Neal and Kobe Bryant are in the finals and down by 20. Do you see Phil Jackson jump in? No. He sits back and coaches;

he sticks to his game plan. So we have formulated a strategy and technique; coaching, training, and motivating daily, encouraging you to take the lead. Whether that's in sports, life, or work, you name it. It is very helpful if you have someone to coach, train, and motivate you to take the Lead in your life. You are the way you see yourself. Are you ready to take the Lead?

CHAPTER 1

Are You The Manager of Your Life or The Leader of Your Life

Often people go through life managing life. They take care of responsibilities. Take care of the basics; most humans fail to reach their true potential because some never choose to take the lead. In life, you're in control of your future; you have to commit to having a command over your life. Once you become the leader of your life, you can enter rooms and doors you wouldn't enter just by managing your life. When managing life, we plan to get through day by day. When we take the Lead, it becomes about multiplying your fruit—leaving an investment that keeps on giving. A leader possesses a vision for their life. A leader is courageous, has integrity, honesty, commitment, humility, and clear focus. A manager controls and oversees things to completion.

I haven't always been the leader in my life. There were times I made decisions that were best for others but not the best for me. I admit there were times I made decisions and done things outside of my character. Without a clear sense of direction, we do what we see or hear. To take the lead, We must transact to transform. I transact with many guests and employees multiple times a day. Make eye contact, Listen, then provide solutions. Transformation is a process. You have to invest daily in who you are. You must study and learn who you are. It would help if you constantly made self-improvements, track your growth, write down your goals and desires, and set deadlines for your purposes. Know your worth—live life with morals and standards. Managing life allows you to become the leader in your life.

What separates a manager from a leader is their ability to take command. A leader sets a vision and wakes up every day with a clear purpose. A leader understands when situations and trouble arise. It's preparation for a more significant challenge. When managing our lives, problems and emergencies will occur. Adapt the mindset that if you came to it, you could get through it. If we haven't corrected the situation correctly, it's bound to repeat itself. As a leader, you create the life you desire; as a manager, you take up the life given to you, and you go through life maintaining. With a curious mind and always wanting to know my purpose, I made many immature decisions. Without a clear sense of purpose, we tend to do what we want. Once you identify your goal, you do things that align with your purpose. You place systems and techniques that allow you to attract the life you deserve. Know that trial and error of life prepared you for this moment. You go from manager to leader when you believe your mentality has to match your beliefs. When you discover who you are, you develop confidence. Take the Lead. Think outside the box.

As a leader, you have to be cautious of what you say and how you do things. As you grow, you will see others around you grow. Leaders create other leaders. In leading, you have to be in the right environment to thrive. Sometimes it takes separation to find your actual ability. During these difficult times in life, we all have been separated and forced to adapt. How has you being separated from the world impacted you? Take the lead and break away from tradition. You have to unlearn to relearn. It takes commitment. You're the way you see yourself; the thoughts we think become our reality. You're a product of your circumstances. Discover your gifts and Take the Lead.

CHAPTER 2

Study Techniques, Be Purposeful

Studying is an essential part of leadership, in which knowledge is acquired. By studying, we see and hear which allows us to learn. It prepares you for what lies ahead. Learning is essential to survival. In learning we pick up techniques. Techniques are what allow you to find efficient ways to get things done. Practices also lead to purpose. Be purposeful in your words and actions. The power of life and death lies between the tongue. We must think and speak positively to attract positive. Before becoming an assistant manager as a cook, I would help fulfill the duties of an assistant manager. I eventually took on the actual role of an assistant manager.

Once I became an assistant, I learned the business, I carried myself as if I was the partner. It's important to know what you do and why, every day you must study and use techniques. Study and research those that are ahead of where you would like to be.

Repetitions bring understanding; the more you do something, the more experience you have of it. Think back from when you were born. You didn't always think well, talk well, walk well; through repetition, you are where you are today. It's only 24 hours a day. Every man has those same 24 hours. The sun is going to rise and set, whether you decide to invest your 24 hours wisely or unwisely. Time waits for no man. You have a gift inside waiting on you to nurture it. By nurturing your talents, it will make room for you to grow. Your gift will allow dominion over your life through studying, using techniques, being purposeful, and nurturing your gift. It would be best if you planned for your success. Plan to prosper. Prosperity is power; power without knowledge is a failure waiting to happen. I say that from experience, not knowing about finances while making $100k, I spent $100k that was coming in. Which resulted in tax trouble with IRS.

No one ever showed me that money was just a tool. Through choices, research, and studying, I realized money is not money until it makes money for you. Think about it? What gifts do you have that you can make life purposeful for you? For me, it was leadership. Everything I've been through or go through is to guide someone else along the journey. There's nothing new under the sun; for every problem or situation you may face, someone else has faced that same problem or situation. It's how you deal with it. I chose to learn, observe, and notice greatness to get the best outcome in all I do.

CHAPTER 3

Who Are You? Why Should You Leave An Investment That Keeps On Giving?

One of the most important questions you face is, who are you? Knowing who you are separates you from others. I'm a leader, helping purpose-driven leaders fulfill life purpose by learning, observing, and noticing greatness. Therefore, every day I must commit to being the best me. It's in finding my purpose I'm able to share what worked for me along the way. Although you will spend the rest of your life learning, every day has a different opportunity. I use my experiences as an example: failed relationship after relationship, overcoming poor eating habits, poor self-control, quitting when things get tough, procrastination and impulsiveness. You name it I have to overcome it. There are many obstacles that are there to help you elevate along your journey. You must know who you are. If not, you will never take the lead in your life. Yes, I've been through a mess; It's now become my message. I've been through pain; it brought me prosperity. I've been tested; those are now my testimonies. Are you feeling me? You know what you've been through, and you understand why now you have to adjust. Are you ready to fully invest in yourself?

Are you ready to take the lead? Why should you invest in yourself? Ask yourself who owe you? That's right, you. Take accountability or responsibility for your life. Commit to it, never make decisions based on emotions from this point forward; use logic. It helps you understand and differentiate between good and bad. You won't always make the best decision. You must learn to honor those. Observing your decision-making is essential in learning who you are, and the reason you are 100% at overcoming bad frustrating days. Love yourself each and every day. By hearing you're able to receive. knowledge that will guide you when you apply it. Many people know that they have a gift. Do they actually nurture the gifts? Are you using your gifts to serve others?

What impact does your gift have on you that you can impact the world? Wealthy people read and think, broke people work and complain. Simple as I summed it up, I never was a reader. Once I was fully convinced, I committed myself. I found myself reading daily through studying and investing. I realized that I had a belief. I acted on my belief. If I can read a book, I can use my expertise and write a resourceful book. There are many people just like you ready to take the lead. Sometimes you may feel I don't know where to start. Leadership is a gift that keeps on giving; just do it. It becomes a thing of the past. In this phase, we must learn, observe, and notice greatness in all we do. Therefore, you know the outcome that you will get; you want a return on your investment. Returns come based on productivity.

CHAPTER 4

Why You Must Train Yourself
To Let Go of Frustration

As soon as you make your mind up, here comes the frustration. Do I want to do this? Am I the person I say I am? Yes, you are. Frustration is needed. Notice, what is frustration? The feeling of being upset or annoyed, mainly because of the inability to do something. Taking the lead requires a change of mindset. There are many times you may not get the results you expect. You may give your best, and your best just may not be good enough to overcome frustration. Life draws things out of you through life experience. The biggest battle we face is the battle within. Most times, the disappointment is more in our heads than in our reality. What's on the inside, it shows up on the outside. Now let's train yourself to overcome frustration by using patience, faith, and gratitude. Understand your life is an example to someone else. Through positive belief, abundance flows; it's not easy to overcome frustration. Trust me, I understand

Through studying and training your thought process enhances. You learn to master your thoughts and emotions better. You become able to identify and observe your frustration. Sometimes it's okay to be frustrated. How you deal with your frustration is what I strive to help you with. Frustration is part of an investment. You don't get frustrated with things you are not investing in.

Investments create expectations; no matter whether it's a person, place, or thing, you're investing in it, because you have an expectation. When you have an expectation, it leads to disappointment. Therefore, when dealing with frustration, we have to be able to identify where it comes from. Mom has always been my biggest supporter, I told her many times I will retire her, I will own my own sonic franchise. I had a whole list of goals that I would just write through my notepad and read. Mom said, "You will never finish anything until you complete things. Your life would never become full circle."

I was not too fond of her response. After a period of disappointment, I felt the frustration. A light bulb went off. You got married before knowing yourself and the other person as well. You played many sports and never went into championships because you didn't put in the work—you are struggling with your finances because you're not planning. You're not hitting goals because you're not setting deadlines. That day impacted me deeply. I learned to set goals. Not only did I set goals and achieve goals, but a couple of my employees also started setting goals, and I started hearing success stories. Some went from renting homes to now they're homeowners. Some went from paying bills, check to check, to now they pay their bills three to six months in advance. Some stopped working for me, opened up their own business, and made significant profits. Some started making better life choices overall.

As I invested in myself, I realized it was essential to share the knowledge and invest in those around me. Knowing what frustrates you and how to let the frustration go not only helps you, but it helps others. It's important to develop positive thinking habits. You should be learning to identify your frustrations by now. Where does the frustration come from?

CHAPTER 5

Drop The Procrastination

Drop the procrastination. Many times I'm asked, how do you manage to achieve things? You say, quickly, stop procrastination. Procrastination is a friend of fear and the enemy of greatness. How about I break that down. I say I want to lose weight. I tell myself everyday , I'm going to the gym . I say that every day because the day before, I thought about it but never acted on it in 30 days; I gained 15 pounds. Versus going to the gym, working out for five minutes the first day. Then going to the gym the next day and doing 10 minutes, before you know it I'm doing 15 minutes for the remaining of the 30 days. The result of that is now I have decreased my weight by 10 pounds. Now I'm on the verge of creating a balanced and healthy lifestyle. Any area of life is no different. You must search for your purpose and do it well. Think about life. You're going to be tested; whether you're ready for the test or not, life is our best classroom. Anything you set out to do, investment and procrastination can arise.

The simple and easy way to overcome procrastination is to do what you said you would do no matter what. Keep in mind if you procrastinated once chances are, you may be caught procrastinating rather than executing your goals and desires. Create systems, schedules, and techniques that allow you to become the best version of yourself. When frustrating moments arise, you have to realize what you need to do to center yourself. Wake up with a purpose and a plan, knowing you are in control of your actions.

Once you realize your purpose, nothing and no one will stand in your way. The more you say you will do things and you complete them, It builds confidence and trust within you. Surrounding yourself with the right people gives you accountability; you have someone to follow up on your goals, communicate with, and build healthy relationships with. Invite those in your life that will push you to be your best.

When I joined ETA, I procrastinated after paying for a program for months, not joining calls I realized I had to join a call. On my first call, I was told never to miss another call. This process is transformational and life-changing. The coach told me, imma get paid if you show up or not. I'm here for you, listen and apply. Don't miss another call. It was through never missing another call. I found my purpose. I understand my worth. I'm in sync with my higher calling. I procrastinated for years on doing something that came naturally. I've become more demanding of myself than others. Based on my personal experience, I know personally what procrastinating for 30 days can do. I want you to list five things you would like to accomplish daily and track your progress. Let's see if we overcome procrastination. It takes 21 consistent days to see a change in the mindset. Thirty-one days to create a habit; our habits determine our future.

CHAPTER 6

What Triggers Frustration

We must know our triggers to overcome any area of our life. You're quickly able to identify and plan a strategy before frustration can arise. You have to know, is it mental or physical? I'm not achieving the results I want. I don't like the shape of my body. I'm not happy with my finances, bills are not being paid on time. I'm not sure where to start when getting my life on track. These are examples of mental frustration. Is it physical? Someone broke into my house; I'm facing abuse, I'm having health issues, getting involved in an accident on the job. These are all examples of physical frustration. Now that we understand physical and mental frustration, how do you choose to identify, and how does your triggers affect you.

When you identify your frustration, you have to reply and know what led to that frustration. Redirect your energy back to the positive. Find a word of gratitude. Once you identify your triggers, you have a choice, remain frustrated or accept the actions that come with the course of that, your life's purpose. Frustrating moments will arise, are you prepared to respond in a positive way. I've had a horrible relationship with my father, but I wanted answers because of him; I am a product of who I became. I did certain things as a man. I acted out because I didn't have the love of my father. I remember I wrote him a letter. Dad I forgive you, I want to know why you treated me in certain ways growing up? I continued to go into great detail about how I felt. I poured my heart out; his response was through a text with blue butterflies. I knew I had carried that hurt and burden for years.

I've been working on techniques and methods to deal with frustration. I identified my frustration and where it came from. I had to forgive. Dad didn't want me to know what his reason was, or it was just he didn't have an answer at the time. Maybe he just didn't have a father to show him how to be a great father. I felt my frustration. I told myself his absence as a father should make me want to be a better father. I'm responsible for learning from his life and become a better product of him. Even though my dad and I don't speak, I use my experience to live and be a better product and be a better man overall. I can be a better father to my kids; whatever I've been through it has allowed me to grow. Sometimes the things that we've been through are placed in our lives to help us grow.

Know your triggers, and once they arise, you have to know how to discontinue them. Heartbreak after heartbreak is what allowed me to triumph. What is one situation that you have been through that will enable you to become the best you? What is one concern that you've been through that has frustrated you, that you felt like you could have done something differently? I want you to create a positive outcome, spend five minutes a day within yourself, fill in how you feel. Let your thoughts, your actions, and your deeds speak to you. Make notes of your triggers. For motivation, develop a positive word of gratitude and redirect your energy. One idea can work for you for the rest of your life. What's that one idea?

CHAPTER 7

Self Inflicted or Outside Influence

Know what's inside and outside of your control. It's important. We are all responsible and accountable for our actions. People are entitled to have a perception. It's great to know how a person feels about you. Most importantly, it matters how you think about yourself. Words carry emotions. If we're not careful or in sync with our emotions, the terms and actions of others can affect our emotions. I have always thought outside the box. I want to know the reason and why do people dream, but don't activate it. People will try to make you feel like you're crazy. They might even call you crazy, retarded, stupid, bipolar. Know that you are none of those things. It's a purpose and a plan created for all lives. You are unique. God has given a specific vision to you. No one has that vision but you. The way you feel about yourself is all in your control.

You will never be able to take control of the opinion of others. Even though some may never admit it, your actions speak volumes. Truth stands alone. Reality is what you believe. Many people have failed to achieve goals, desires, or live a purposeful life because of what someone else said. Do you know why that happened? Somewhere their purpose and opinion matter more than the opinion of your own, or what that person said is correct, and therefore you never believe in your ability to prosper. I was told at 17 years old; I was going to end up flipping burgers. I'll never be successful. Guess what? That was outside influence. I knew what I was capable of, what I've accomplished. Not only did I end up flipping burgers, but I also ended up a partner. I went from making an hourly rate to getting paid by a percentage. I went from being counted out to counted on. Self-belief, determination, and faith changes a mindset.

When I'm told I can't do something, I tell myself I can. When I'm told I can do something, I tell myself, just because I can, doesn't mean I should. Never allow the belief of others to become your belief. It's great to surround yourself with the right people. I'm in the room with successful people and one thing sticks out to me is they never talk about people or what's going on. They are always talking about ideas and solutions to what's going on. What conversations do you have daily? What influence do the people around you have on you? Spend the next days reflecting on your impact and the power you have on others. Dedicate life to taking care of what's in your control. What's outside of your control is already controlled.

CHAPTER 8

Why Is It Important To Study Something and Someone Daily

As humans, we learn by watching and listening. Once you identify the direction of your life, it's important to study something or someone on your path daily. Achieving a high level of success requires a system and proven techniques. Through researching, analyzing, you will come across methods, and concepts. Whatever area of life you're looking to achieve success in, it is no different. It starts with preparation and planning. Preparation is a process of being made ready. A plan is a detailed proposal of getting things done. As a business owner, I study leadership and business daily. I want to know how others became successful. I want to know what their struggles were? What is their background? What and how did they come across problems? Most of all, I wanted to know how did they develop solutions? No matter what you choose to do, it's always a problem. Most likely, everyone sees the problem. People want solutions. As a leader of a fast food restaurant, every day, I must provide answers. Guests stop by because they want food. Not just any food, they want quality. We're not a fine dining restaurant. They want speed. Last but not least, they want accuracy. Guests want what they paid for. Guests want someone to go above and beyond to make them feel appreciated. They could have chosen any restaurant. They could have chosen to eat anywhere. By delivering consistent quality, speed, and accuracy, I created raving fans. I have guests that would stop by the drive-in four or five times a day. I managed to drive an impact of sales over 52%. Two hundred thousand plus in back-to-back drive-ins. Recognized as 2018 turn around operator of the year within the DLR franchise. Becoming a better me, I displayed a positive attitude. I expect a positive outcome. When dealing with people, I learned to accept them for who they are. The way I carry myself can affect others. The power of life and death comes from the tongue. Overcoming frustration is a choice. The more I thought productive, the more productive I became. The more I coached, train, and motivated those around me; my job became more manageable.

I went from working 70 to 85 hours a week to a normal 40 to 45-hour workweek. Some weeks I worked maybe 20 hours. Without the proper training and preparation, you shouldn't expect to take the lead. Success is not just going to arise. Every day you must train yourself and prepare for your success. Remember, studying is essential to your growth. It must be a part of your everyday process. I'm attending weekly accountability calls with high-profile leaders to achieve and excel at a high level. Setting attainable stretch goals weekly. Find and engage with people that will stretch you to grow. Use your resources wisely. Uniquely be you; spend the next 30 days focusing on one area of your life where you would like to see growth. Study something, and study somebody daily in your desired space. Powerful action that's sticks with me from my mentor Dr. Eric Thomas, execution is worshiped. We must be more demanding of ourselves more than others.

CHAPTER 9

Accountability Comes From Within

Many times we often wonder why we are not achieving the level of success we want. It's you; the responsibility comes from within. You should never expect someone else to care more about your life than you. You are obtaining a gift and favor on your life. You are responsible for nurturing and developing your skill. Remember, there are always resources, connections, and people to help guide you along your life journey. Life is a journey of self-discovery through experiences. Have you discovered what you need to take accountability? For me, it was taking command and control over my life. I learned that for me to give my best, I had to be my best. Daily I face myself in the mirror. I have to be able to deal with myself to deal with anyone. People want to see you do good, Some just not better than them. What matters most is what you want. I wanted to become the best version of myself. Every challenging situation in my life, I created that. The result of my choices created my daily circumstances. I admitted to myself I don't have a problem with making decisions. I have a problem with making poor decisions. I realize the choices I make today will affect the way I live ten years from now. By becoming a better version of me, I can now help you become a better you. It's not about what you have; it's about what you do with what you have. Ten years as a business owner, I overcame many failures.

It is accountable to take responsibility for my actions, decisions, and words. I have experienced my darkest days. I've been torn down. I embraced it. I smiled, the accountability came from within. Every day I wake up, it's a new start. I said in my mind, my best day would not compare to my worst day. Learn the power of observation, pay attention to detail, learn to speak greatness to the inner man. The man that knows life has a purpose and a plan. The excuse is over the wait is over; you passed all of the tests. Character is the cornerstone to your success; Competence will keep you growing and thriving. Purpose-driven leaders will never forget excellence. Someone is always watching you, even though you might not know it.

You're an inspiration to someone and because you took accountability. The people around you will take responsibility. The people you hang around with determining your future. Who are you surrounding yourself with? You can't be the only one with the knowledge and expertise.We all have someone we look up to. They have someone they look up to. All things are connected. Are you where you want to be in life, be honest with yourself? Are you the leader of your life? What area of your life must you accept accountability for you to thrive? Greatness is connected to responsibility.

CHAPTER 10

A Better Day For Yourself
By Being Genuine To You

Be genuine to yourself. At this point, it doesn't matter what you've done or what someone else has done. Be authentic to you, Love and cherish you. Look at yourself in the mirror and love that person that you see in the mirror. You inspire many. We often become blind to the greatness that lies within because of our inability to be genuine to ourselves. Nothing and no one comes before you. If you can't do for yourself, how could you do for another? I will spend quality time alone. I have chosen to get in sync with my thoughts and emotions. My intuition guides me; it speaks to the soul. It knows its purpose. I'm embracing the time doing things that makes life meaningful. The memories I've created still last forever. At the end of the day, what have you done to impact the world? We're here to multiply our fruit, enhance, and serve one another. Self-preservation is a law of nature. Everything in life connects in some sort. Everything you experience is to help you along your journey. Taking proper care of yourself will teach others how to properly learn to care for themselves. It allows others to respect you. Respect is earned, not given. People respect those who appreciate themselves. If you treat yourself with a high level of care, others will see and value that.

Be decisive in your thought process. Own up to allowing yourself to live life on your terms, mean what you say, say what you mean. You are a value, which means you must live by principles and standards. Success is desired by many, obtained by few. Everyone wants to be successful until it's time to be demanding. Your future success depends on today's decisions. You are unique and fearfully made. You are full of love and care which allows you to replenish your spirit. Serve others with your overflow. An empty vessel can't serve. Caring for self is essential to the act of survival. Being genuine to yourself is how you take your power back. Blaming others puts them in a position to have the ability to control your actions. Spend time and focus on building the new you. From this point forward, imagine the best version of yourself and show up as the best version of yourself. Be genuine to yourself, and love who you are every day, the same way you would do someone else. You are equipped to take the lead. The choice is yours. Take The Lead. Tap into your power by overcoming frustration.

About The Author

Tracey Jones is a profound author, ETA Certified Speaker and business owner.

Tracey grew up in Monroe, La, also known as "gun-roe." He experienced pain, trauma, and hardships at an early age. Determined not to be a product of his environment, Tracey had to overcome custody battles between his mother and father, neighborhood homicides, and a community saturated with drugs.

During his senior year in high school, he lost his Aunt, and lost his way. He didn't graduate with his senior class and ended up getting expelled from college for trying to sell drugs, and lost his baseball scholarship in the process. The loss of a baseball scholarship landed him back working at Sonic.

In 2011 Tracey took over his first Sonic Drive-In as an operating partner. He immediately impacted sales and profits. Working long hours daily, and being the only person with the knowledge and expertise, quickly lead to frustration. Tracey realized life isn't about what you know, it's about how well you can teach and train others. Tracey became **focused on executing** and achieving results at a high level by impacting his team first.

His drive and dedication put him **in a position to take the lead** in his life. Tracey helps purpose-driven leaders learn the power of observation, and paying attention to detail, to fulfill their purpose as leaders. Tracey's goal is to impact and change one billion lives through coaching, training, and motivating. Tracey knows that **studying is essential to growth, and learning is necessary for survival.**

Tracey is also the founder of L.O.N.G. Leaders Of The Next Generation, a non-profit, Which was inspired by a youth conversation with his first cousin. In 2021, Tracey became a certified Eric Thomas & Associates Speaker. Take the Lead is Tracey's first book.

You can contact Tracey Jones by visiting Traceydjones.com

www.ingramcontent.com/pod-product-compliance
Lightning Source LLC
Chambersburg PA
CBHW031227090426
42740CB00007B/737